GRADE 1

who what where

when FLASH how

FORWARD

READING

fact opinion

Written by Kerrie Baldwin

Illustrations by John Haslam

D1306580

Flash Kids
Spark Publishing

Spark Publishing
A Division of Barnes & Noble
120 Fifth Avenue
New York, NY 10011
www.sparknotes.com

ISBN-13: 978-1-4114-0703-9
ISBN-10: 1-4114-0703-2

For more information, please visit *www.flashkidsbooks.com*
Please submit changes or report errors to *www.flashkidsbooks.com/errors*

Printed and bound in the United States

1 3 5 7 9 10 8 6 4 2

Dear Parent,

As your child encounters higher levels of reading difficulty, it is vital that he or she not only follows along with the text, but also understands the meaning of what is being read. Comprehension is often very difficult for young readers, but practice is proven to develop it. Here to help your child with reading comprehension skills are almost 100 pages of fun and entertaining short stories of interest to first-graders.

This colorful workbook features entertaining readings followed by activities that will help your child focus on key skills such as: who, what, where, when, why, and how; determining the sequence of events; and identifying the meaning of vocabulary words in context. He or she will practice a range of test-taking formats, too—from matching words and pictures to using word banks.

The activities are designed for your child to handle alone, but you can read along and help with any troublesome words, ideas, or questions. Patience is key for reading comprehension. Then together you can check answers at the back of the workbook, and you should always give praise and encouragement for his or her effort. In addition, try to find other ways for your child to practice reading comprehension. You can leave a note that describes what fun activities you and your child will do first, second, and third that day. Later, have your child read a bedtime story to you, and then ask him or her some questions about it. Remember that reading is everywhere, so just use your imagination!

Mess in the Morning

Anna gets a special breakfast today! Anna's dad will make pancakes and eggs. He puts the milk and pancake mix on the table. He turns around too fast. His elbow hits the milk! Anna sees the milk spill onto the floor. Their cat licks it up. Anna is sad. She won't eat pancakes today. But Anna's dad cooks eggs. He makes some toast, too. He puts strawberry jelly on her toast. Anna loves strawberries! She had a great breakfast after all.

Read each question. Circle the right picture.

1. Who made breakfast?

2. What did Anna's dad spill?

3. What did Anna eat for breakfast?

Dressing for the Day

José looks out his bedroom window. He watches leaves fall from the trees. Some are red. Some are yellow. Some are orange. This is José's favorite time of year. He loves to play in the leaves. But José needs to get dressed. He puts on jeans and a sweater. He puts socks and shoes on his feet. Then José puts on his fall coat. His sister stops him at the front door. She gives him mittens. He puts them on his hands. Now José is ready to play!

Draw a line from each word to its matching picture.

coat

mittens

shoes

Playing in the Park

The sun is shining on the grass. The air is warm. It's a great day! Tyler's family walks to the park. Everyone there is having fun. There are people riding bikes. Some kids are jumping rope. Tyler runs to the swings. He rides a swing and feels the wind. Tyler can see his sister. She and her friend are playing catch. Little Grace misses the ball! Tyler can see his parents, too. They are sitting on a blanket. His mom opens the picnic basket. It must be time for lunch!

Circle the picture that shows each sentence.

1. Tyler rides the swing.

2. The girls play catch.

3. Mom and Dad set up the picnic.

About Robins

Have you ever seen a robin? A robin is a bird with an orange chest. It has a yellow beak. Watch for robins in the morning. You could see one hopping on the ground. It could be looking for worms to eat. Or it could be looking for small sticks. Robins use sticks to make nests. Their nests are up in trees. Nests keep a robin's eggs safe. The eggs are a pretty blue. What will happen when the eggs open? You will see baby robins!

Match each picture to its name. Write the word. Use the words in the word bank.

egg   robin   nest

1. _____

2. _____

3. _____

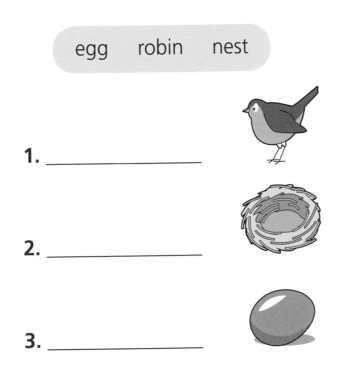

Pretty Picture

Jenna wants to make a picture for her grandmother. She takes paper and crayons outside. Jenna sits under a tree in her yard. She looks at her house. The front door is red. The roof of the house is brown. Jenna uses the red crayon and the brown crayon. She draws her house. She takes the green crayon next. She makes short lines. It is easy to draw grass! Then she looks up at the sky. It is all blue. She uses the blue crayon to color the sky. Jenna runs inside. Her grandmother loves the picture!

What crayons did Jenna use? Draw a line from each word to its color.

grass

roof

sky

Sleepy Pets

The house next door is fun. There are four kids and four pets! The kids are playing tag in the backyard today. Sometimes the dog tries to play, too! Everyone laughs. But soon everyone is tired. The dog goes to its doghouse. It lays down. The kids go inside their home. The cat is chasing the bird in the kitchen! They catch the bird and put it in its cage. The fish is safe in its bowl. Everyone can take a nap now.

Where do they sleep?
Draw a line from each pet to its home.

New Baby

Nicholas heard that Mrs. Richards had a baby! The baby's name is Kayla. Mrs. Richards brought Kayla home yesterday. Nicholas wants to see the baby. He picks some flowers from the garden. He ties them together. This will be a nice present. He walks down the street to the Richards' house. Mr. Richards answers the door. He is holding Kayla. She is so small! She looks very warm in her yellow blanket. Nicholas goes inside. He gives the flowers to Mrs. Richards. She lets him hold the baby. Kayla falls asleep in his arms!

Read each question. Circle the right picture.

1. Who did Mrs. Richards bring home?

2. What does Nicholas bring?

3. What is Kayla wearing?

Your Own Tomatoes

You can grow tomatoes! Find a very sunny place. It could be near a window or outside. Plant tomato seeds in some dirt. Give the seeds water. Watch the green plant grow! Soon you will see green balls on the plant. These are tomatoes. But they need to ripen. They will change from green to yellow to orange to red. Then you can pick them. You can eat them right off the plant. Or you can cut them up. Make a salad. You could make salsa or tomato sauce, too. Tomatoes taste so good!

Draw a line from each sentence to its matching picture.

He is watering seeds.

It is a ripening tomato.

He is making sauce.

Digging in the Dirt

Zack helps in the garden. He likes getting dirty! He wants to plant some flowers. He gets on his knees. He digs a small hole. Then Zack places a pink flower in the hole. He pats the dirt around the flower. This will hold the flower still. Then Zack gives the flower some water. He asks his mother what he should plant now. She is pulling weeds out of a flowerbed. They see something run by very fast. Zack thinks it was a rabbit! They see a hole in the vegetable garden. The rabbit took a carrot!

Look at each picture. Draw a line under the right sentence.

1.

Zack plants a flower.

Zack walks his dog.

2.

His mom watches the bird fly.

His mom pulls out weeds.

3.

The rabbit is taking a carrot!

The cat is taking a carrot!

Emma's Job

"Cock-a-doodle-doo!" The rooster is loud! Emma wakes up. It's time for work. Emma jumps out of bed. She can't wait to see her animal friends. Her job is to feed them. She will feed the horses first. Emma brings some hay to the stable. The horses are very happy to see her. Next she puts some pig food in the ditch. The pigs dive in. Then Emma takes the cows to the big field. The cows eat the grass slowly. Emma and the cows watch the sun rise. She loves living on a farm!

Where do the animals eat? Draw a line from each animal to its eating-place.

cow

pig

horse

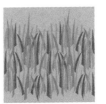

Zoo Trip

Today is the class trip to the zoo. Mia is happy to see many animals! The white polar bears look very soft. The parrots are colorful and loud. Next they see the animals from Africa. These animals live in a special place in the zoo. It has grass and trees just like in Africa. The class watches a gray elephant drink water. Behind the elephant is a baby elephant! There are three giraffes, too. Their necks are very long. Mia hears noises up in a tree. It's a monkey!

What is it? Draw a line from each animal to its name.

elephant

monkey

giraffe

Bee Buzz

"Buzz! Buzz!" Do you hear the bee? Can you see it? The bee flies in the air. It has black and yellow stripes. Watch the bee land on a flower. The bee is eating the flower's nectar. Now the bee is full and sleepy. It's time for the bee to go home. It flies to the hive. There are a lot of bees there! Some bees are making honey. They talk to each other, too. They talk by dancing! Bees are very busy bugs. But you shouldn't trouble a hive. Then a bee might sting you.

Read each question. Circle the right picture.

1. What does a bee make?

2. What gives food to bees?

3. Who might the bees sting?

At the Store

Ethan's dad shops for food every week. Sometimes Ethan goes with him. All the food looks so good! Ethan wants to get cookies and ice cream only. But his dad says no. They need food for breakfast, lunch, and dinner, too. Ethan points to some red apples. His dad tells him to pick good ones. They shouldn't have soft spots. Next Ethan takes two carrots. That's not enough. His dad takes two more. Then Ethan gets milk. Check the date! The milk is safe to drink. Ethan learns a lot from his dad!

What did Ethan and his dad buy? Write the name of each food.
Use the words in the word bank.

apples   carrots   milk

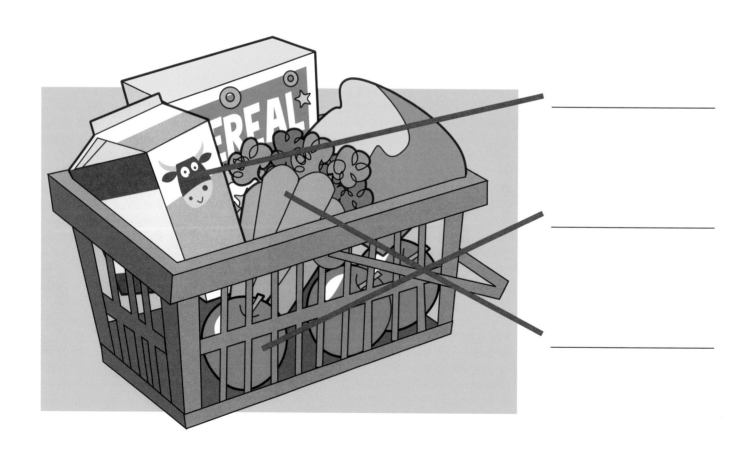

Cool Cookout

There is a big cookout at Jacob's house. Many family members come over. The adults cook outside. The kids play all day long. Jacob wants to play with water balloons. He tells his sister Abigail. She finds balloons and fills them with water. Jacob finds Connor. He is Jacob's cousin. Connor loves water balloons! Jacob, Abigail, and Connor throw the balloons at each other. Splash! Splash! Two balloons hit Jacob. Aunt Nicole says it is time for lunch. Jacob should dry off first!

Read each question. Circle the right answer.

1. Who is Jacob's sister?

        Abigail   Erin   Jordan

2. What is the name of Jacob's cousin?

        Jordan   Connor   Samuel

3. Who got wet?

        Connor   Aunt Nicole   Jacob

Cleaning Day

Mom wakes up Lauren. It's cleaning day! Lauren gets ready to do chores. She finds a clean rag. She wipes up the dust in her room. There is a lot of dust. Lauren goes downstairs to the kitchen. Where's the broom? She finds one in the corner. Lauren uses the broom to sweep crumbs off the floor. Then she takes a sponge. She washes the dishes in the sink. She is working hard. Mom says she is doing a good job. Lauren sees a peanut butter sandwich on the table. It's time for lunch!

What did Lauren use?
Draw a line from each chore to its matching tool.

wash dishes   broom

dust   sponge

sweep floor   rag

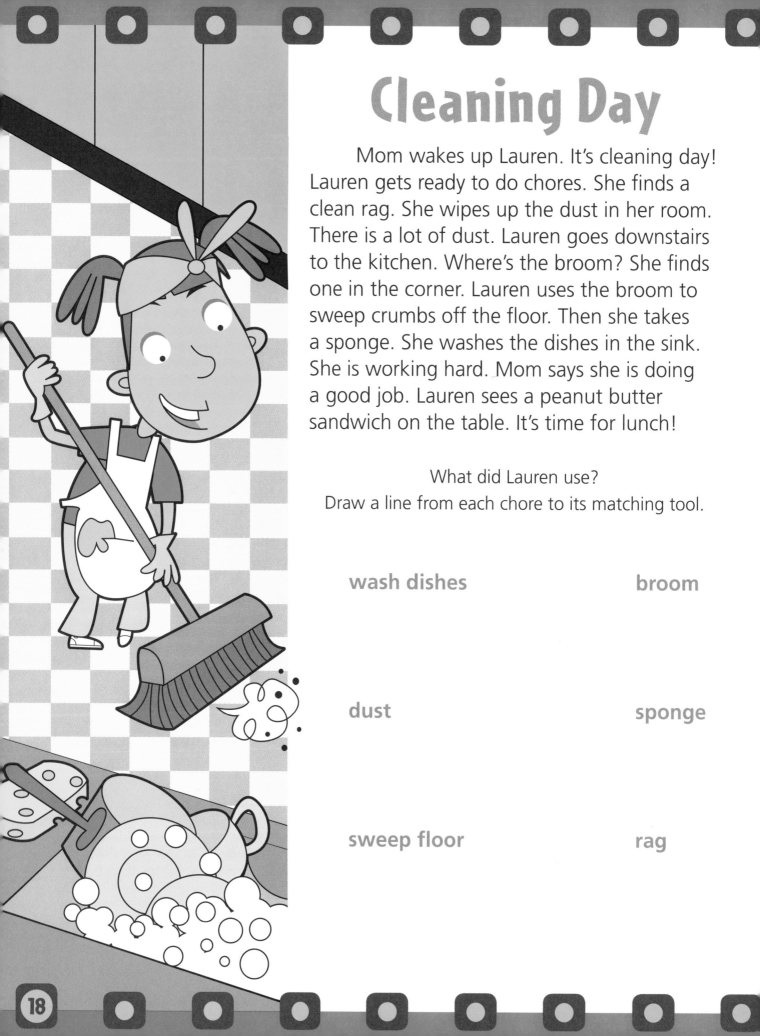

Home, Sweet Home

Where do you live? Do you live in the country? You might live in a house. Your house might be on a farm. Do you live in a city? You may live in a tall building. Your home would be one of the apartments inside. There are many kinds of homes. Did you know that you could live on the water? Some people live inside boats. Their homes can go from place to place. Some people live in places with only snow and ice. Where do those people live? They make igloos out of ice blocks!

Answer the questions below. Use the words in the word bank.

igloo   boat   apartment

1. What home is part of a building? _____

2. What home is made of ice blocks? _____

3. What home can float on water? _____

Batter Up!

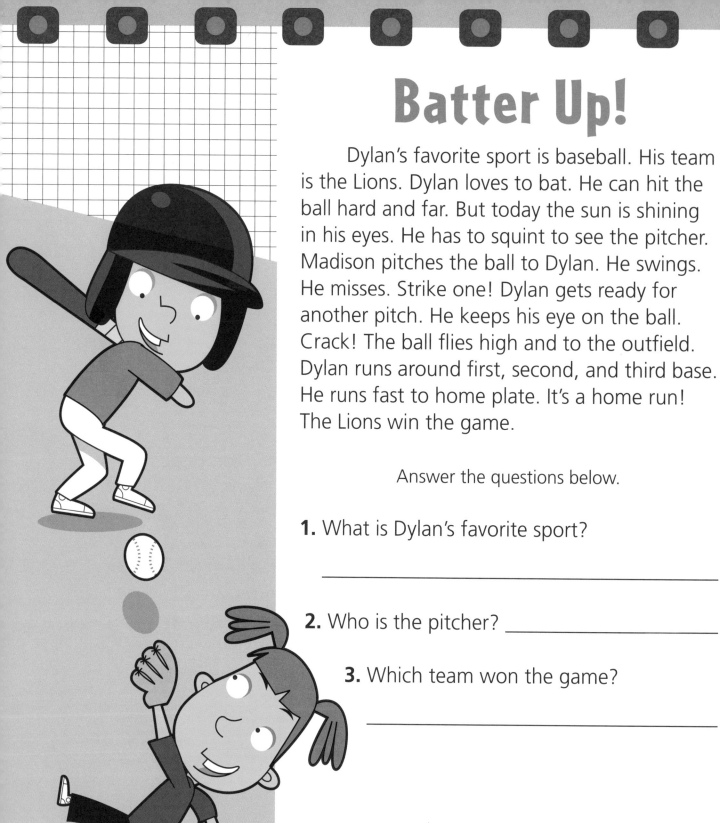

Dylan's favorite sport is baseball. His team is the Lions. Dylan loves to bat. He can hit the ball hard and far. But today the sun is shining in his eyes. He has to squint to see the pitcher. Madison pitches the ball to Dylan. He swings. He misses. Strike one! Dylan gets ready for another pitch. He keeps his eye on the ball. Crack! The ball flies high and to the outfield. Dylan runs around first, second, and third base. He runs fast to home plate. It's a home run! The Lions win the game.

Answer the questions below.

1. What is Dylan's favorite sport?

_____

2. Who is the pitcher? _____

3. Which team won the game?

_____

Trick or Treat

Halloween is here! Olivia dresses up like a clown. She puts on a rainbow wig. Her father paints her face, too. Her brother Benjamin dresses up like a crocodile. He sees out the crocodile's mouth! Olivia and Benjamin are trick-or-treating tonight. They ring doorbells and people give them candy. Halloween is a very fun holiday. They go home and empty their bags. Olivia has twenty pieces of candy. Benjamin has two more pieces. He gives one piece to Olivia. Now they have the same number. Benjamin is a nice brother!

Read each question. Circle the right answer.

1. Who dressed up like a clown?

Olivia   Michael   James

2. What was Benjamin for Halloween?

horse   crocodile   airplane

3. Who got the most candy?

Benjamin   Olivia   Luis

Lunch Munch

The lunchroom is loud. Kids are talking in the lunch line. They are hungry. They want to pick their lunches. Today's lunch is pasta with sauce on top or a cheese sandwich. They both sound good! The kids sit down at the long tables. You can hear them talking and laughing. Everyone is eating, too. Sometimes a fork falls to the floor. Oops! Later the kids go back in line. It's time for a sweet treat. Today there are cookies. A cookie tastes great with milk. Yum!

What tastes good?
Draw a line between foods that go together.

bread	cookie
milk	sauce
pasta	cheese

Tree Talk

Trees are almost everywhere. They are the tallest living things. Some trees are very old. They can live longer than a person. But many trees are cut down. Sometimes a whole forest of trees is gone. Why? We use the wood to make new paper. But birds live in trees. People are taking away their homes! They have to look for new trees. Sometimes a new forest is very far away. People need to stop cutting down so many trees.

Answer the questions below.

1. What is made up of many trees?

_____

2. What can people make from trees?

_____

3. Who lives in trees? _____

Sunday Hike

Brooke goes hiking every Sunday. Her father takes her to the hiking trails. The hills are rocky. It's easy to slip and fall. They wear boots to help them climb. Look! There's a chipmunk! They stop to watch nature. Brooke wants to remember all the plants and animals. She opens her backpack. She takes out her notebook and writes in it. Then Brooke and her father are hungry. They eat some fruit and nuts. He tells Brooke about the hardest thing he ever climbed. It was a mountain!

Answer the questions below. Use the words in the word bank.

mountain   boots   backpack

1. What does Brooke wear on her feet? _____

2. What does she carry her notebook in? _____

3. What is the hardest thing that Brooke's father ever climbed?

_____

Great Games

It's time to play outside! This is the best part of the school day. The class runs out in the grass. Jennifer has a big ball. "Let's play kickball!" She starts a team of girls. David gets a team of boys to play with them. More kids play on the hardtop. Brian and Cameron jump rope. They race to see who jumps faster. Maria finds a piece of yellow chalk. She draws hopscotch squares on the ground. Paige goes first. She jumps from square to square. Everyone has fun!

Who was playing the games? Draw a line between each game and the matching names.

kickball   Maria and Paige

hopscotch   Brian and Cameron

jump rope   Jennifer and David

Matt's Birthday

Matt turned seven years old on Saturday. He had a birthday party! Friends and family came. Everyone wore party hats. Matt's hat was striped with blue and yellow. He opened the present from Grandpa first. It was a basketball! Alexander and Sophie played basketball with him. Next it was time for cake. Everyone sang "Happy Birthday" to Matt. He blew on the seven candles. They stayed lit. He blew again. They wouldn't blow out. His mom used trick candles! Everyone laughed. Then they helped him blow them out.

Read each question. Circle the right answer.

1. What day was Matt's party?

Friday   Wednesday   Saturday

2. Who gave Matt a new basketball?

Grandpa   Alexander   Sophie

3. What did everyone laugh at?

presents   hats   candles

Colorful Cats

"Meow!" Do you hear the cat? Do you have one? Have you seen a cat? Cats come in many colors. They can be black, white, gray, orange, or striped. Sometimes a black cat has white paws. It looks like the cat is wearing socks! Cats make great pets. They are happy when you rub their fur. They like to chase things, too. Baby cats are extra playful. They are called kittens. A kitten is small and fuzzy when it's born. But it will grow up to be a big cat!

Answer the questions below. Use the words in the word bank.

white   kitten   meow

1. What sound do cats make? _____

2. What is one color that a cat can be? _____

3. What is a baby cat called? _____

Reading Like a Rabbit

    All the kids like Mr. Martin. He is a good teacher. Every Friday Mr. Martin lets the class read anything they want. Some kids bring books. Others bring comic books! Today Hailey is reading a story. She reads about a turtle and a rabbit. They are having a race. The rabbit falls asleep! Hailey learns that being slow isn't always bad. You just need to keep going. The turtle wins the race! She puts down the story. Some kids are asleep. They thought they had time for a nap. They are just like the rabbit!

Answer the questions below.

1. Who is Hailey's teacher? _____

2. What is Hailey reading? _____

3. Who wins the race? _____

Full of Food

Do you like Thanksgiving? Caleb doesn't. He thinks that turkey is boring. Even Grandma's stuffing doesn't taste so good. Why does Mom bake a pie made of pumpkins? Caleb wants cherry pie instead. What does he eat at Thanksgiving dinner? Cranberry sauce! He puts a lot on his plate. But Caleb doesn't want to hurt Grandma's feelings. He takes a little of the other food. Later he gets more cranberry sauce. He is very full now. His brother Ryan wants to play football after dinner. Caleb feels too sick to play. He wants to sleep. Maybe next year he will eat other foods, too.

Read each question. Circle the right answer.

1. What does Caleb like to eat best?

turkey   cranberry sauce   pumpkin pie

2. Who made the stuffing?

Grandma   Mom   Ryan

3. What does Caleb do after dinner?

play football   read   sleep

Tricky Skis

Swish! Swish! Brianna watches other kids ski down the big hill. This is her first time on a snowy mountain. Her family is there on a trip. This is the winter break from school. They are learning how to ski. Brianna keeps falling! It isn't easy to walk with skis on your feet. She gets very cold, too. Brianna can't wait to go back inside. She can warm up near the fireplace. She remembers that today is Tuesday. They will go home tomorrow. She has to tell her friends about her trip. Brianna wants to ski before the trip is over. She will try extra hard.

Read each question. Circle the right picture or word.

1. Where did Brianna go on a trip?

2. What did she do there?

3. When will she go home?

Tuesday   **Wednesday**   **Thursday**

Truth About Trains

How fast is a train? It can go faster than a boat. A train is even faster than a car. But it is so long and heavy. How can a train move so quickly? The train's wheels are on tracks. The tracks are very smooth. This helps the wheels turn extra fast. The train has a lot of power, too. The person who drives the train is called the conductor. The conductor tells the train how fast it should go. He also calls people to get on the train. The conductor blows a whistle. The sound is high and loud. The train is going to start moving. "All aboard!"

Answer the questions below. Use the words in the word bank.

tracks   conductor   whistle

1. Who drives the train? _____

2. What does the conductor blow? _____

3. Where do the wheels roll? _____

Hide-and-Seek

It is Ashley's turn to find her friends. They are playing hide-and-seek in her backyard. Ashley closes her eyes. She counts to ten. She hears her friends laughing. She opens her eyes. She can't see much. The sun is already gone. She calls to her friends to come out. She walks through the grass. A bush scratches her arm. Thump! Ashley falls. She lands on Leah! Leah was hiding behind a bush. The game is over. Jack was under the table. Gavin was hiding in the tool shed. They picked some good hiding places.

Where did they hide?
Draw a line from each person to his or her hiding place.

Leah

Gavin

Jack

Late!

Sean looks at his watch. It shows 4:00. Oh no! He should be at the pool. Sean has swimming practice today. He forgot that today is Thursday. He needs to hurry! Sean puts his swim shorts in his backpack. He gets on his bike. He starts pedaling very fast. His heart is thumping. He parks his bike in front of school. He runs inside. His shoes squeak. He races to the pool. He sees his dad. His dad is glad that Sean is okay. But he tells Sean to hurry up and get in the pool. Sean's dad is the swimming teacher!

Read each question. Circle the right picture or word.

1. Where is Sean going?

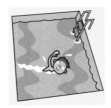

2. When is practice?

3. Who was waiting for Sean?

Dad   Mom   Grandpa

Molly the Monkey

Molly the monkey has many friends to visit. Some of her friends are monkeys. Some are other animals. They all live in the jungle. Molly swings to the next tree. The parrot is there. He is red, yellow, and blue. He loves to talk. Then Molly swings down to the ground. She almost walks into the spider's web. "Sorry, spider!" Next Molly wanders to the jungle river. She sees her friend the lizard. She is sunbathing on a rock. Molly rests at the edge of the river. It begins to get dark. Molly walks inside a big cave. She looks up. Her friends the bats are just waking up. But it's time for Molly to sleep!

Where do they live? Draw a line from each animal to its home.

spider

parrot

bat

lizard

Elephant Trunks

Elephants are one of the biggest animals. Their ears look like huge fans. They live in very hot places. How do they stay cool? They use their long trunks to suck in water and spray it on themselves. A trunk is a very long nose. But it can do more than smell! The trunk brings water to the elephant's mouth for drinking. It pulls up grass, too. An elephant couldn't eat without a trunk. Elephants also use their trunks to hug each other. Two elephants twist their trunks together! Trunks can be very loud. They make noises like a horn. This is how elephants call other elephants. A trunk is faster than a telephone!

Look at each picture. Draw a line under the right sentence.

1.

The elephant lives a long time.

The elephant splashes water to keep cool.

2.

Elephants hug with their trunks.

Elephants hug with their tails.

3.

Its trunk makes loud noises.

Elephants can live in the jungle.

Clowns in Town

Evan loves the circus. His brother Tom does, too. Their dad drives them to the circus. Evan and Tom go to the ticket booth first. The price is five dollars. Evan finds the money in his pocket. Tom pays, too. Then they look at the sign. The clown show is in the big tent. Evan and Tom run to the tent. The show is starting! The clowns are good at juggling. They are so funny! They play tricks on each other. One clown slips on a banana peel. But he is not hurt. It's silly! The show ends and Evan looks at his watch. It says 5:00. It's time to go home. Maybe Evan and Tom will play like clowns after dinner!

Read each question. Circle the right picture or word.

1. Who goes to the circus with Evan?

Trevor   Steve   Tom

2. What does Evan pay?

3. Where is the clown show?

4. When do they leave the circus?

5:00   1:00   10:00

Castle Contest

Morgan and Danny are going to the beach. But they don't want to swim in the water. They are going to play with the sand. Danny and Morgan will make castles with it! Today is the big contest. The best sand castle wins a prize. Morgan has a great idea for a tall sand castle. She fills a pail with water. The water will hold the sand together. Then Morgan pushes the sand into piles. She makes a castle with three towers. Morgan works fast. The castles need to be done by 2:30. She puts a flag in the top. Danny's castle is big, too. But Morgan wins the contest! Her prize is a goldfish.

Answer the questions below.

1. Where is the contest?

_____

2. What are the castles made of?

_____

3. When must the castles be done?

_____

4. Who wins the contest?

_____

Pond Pals

You can see many animals at the pond. You may see ducks there. Ducks are birds. They like to float on top of the water. Do you see a green frog nearby? Is the frog also floating on the water? It is sitting on a plant. This flat leaf is called a lily pad. The lily pad lives in the pond, too. Look at the edge of the pond. Look close at the grass. Is something crawling? It's a snail. It is slow. But there is a fast animal in the pond. It lives under the water. Do you see it swimming? It's a fish!

Draw a line from each sentence to its matching picture.

It is floating on water.

It is sitting on a lily pad.

It is crawling on grass.

It is swimming underwater.

Soccer Star

Jon puts on his soccer uniform. He feels a little sad. This is the last game! He really wants to win. Jon meets his team on the grassy field. He can't kick the soccer ball out of the field, or his team could lose. Jon is careful. He only uses his feet to move the ball. Jon kicks it hard. The black and white ball flies through the air! It lands on the other end of the field. The other team tries to stop the ball. But it is rolling too fast. Will it go into the goal? The goalie reaches out. He is the one player who can use his hands. He misses. The ball is in the goal. Jon's team wins the game!

Answer the questions below. Use the words in the word bank.

goalie   foot   field   today

1. When is the last game? _____

2. What does Jon use to kick the ball? _____

3. Where does the ball need to stay? _____

4. Who can touch the ball with his hands? _____

Day at the Office

Today is Take Your Daughter to Work Day. Samantha doesn't have to go to school! She will be at Mom's office instead. Mom drives them in her car. The roads are very busy. Many people drive into the big city. Mom tells Samantha to look up. The buildings are so tall here! There must be a hundred floors in that one. That's where Mom works. They go to Mom's office and sit at her desk. Samantha learns what Mom does all day. Soon it's time for lunch. The sidewalks are snowy. They want to eat hot soup. Mom will take Samantha to a shop after lunch. Mom and Samantha have a fun day together!

Read each question. Circle the right picture or word.

1. What took Samantha to the city?

2. When did she go there?

3. Who showed Samantha the tall buildings?

Mom   Dad   her sister

4. Where will she go after lunch?

home   a shop   the airport

Moving Away

Diego and Tony see each other every day. They live on the same street. Diego and Tony are best friends. But today Diego has some sad news. He tells Tony that his family is moving tomorrow. They have a new house in Springfield. They won't see each other every day anymore. The new house is too far to walk to. But Diego says the house has a lot of rooms. It also has an extra big yard. Diego and Tony will have more space for playing. Tony can come to the new house on Saturday. They will still be best friends!

Answer the questions below.

1. Who is moving to a new house? _____

2. Where is he moving? _____

3. When can Tony visit? _____

4. Will Diego and Tony still be friends? _____

Cooking in the Kitchen

Uncle Robert is making dinner. His family is coming over to eat. He needs to make a lot of food. Uncle Robert needs to start! He turns on the oven. Then he puts the chicken in the oven. The time is 4:30. Uncle Robert should cook the rolls next. He makes little balls of bread. He puts the rolls in the oven at 5:00. Now he cuts up the carrots. Uncle Robert likes to make carrot circles. He checks the time. The clock says 5:30. It's time to cook them. He drops the carrots in a pot of hot water. Everything is cooking. Ding-dong! Uncle Robert opens the door. His family comes inside. "It smells wonderful in here!" they say.

When is it cooked? Draw a line from each food to a clock.

Know About Snow

What is falling from the sky? It's white and fluffy. It must be snow! Snow can fall any time it's cold outside. It usually falls in the winter. It falls most often in the north, where it gets very cold. Snow is made when water in the clouds turns to ice. Pieces of ice come together. These pieces are called snowflakes. The snowflakes fall from the clouds to the ground. Have you seen snowflakes up close? Each one has a different shape. When many fall together, they can make big piles of snow. It is fun to play in the snow! You can make large balls of snow. Put them in a pile. Add a hat on top. It's a snowman!

Read each question. Circle the right answer.

1. What is snow made of?

ice   glass   candy

2. When does snow fall?

summer   winter   never

3. Where is the most snow?

south   west   north

4. What can you make with balls of snow?

snowflake   snowman   mailman

Madeline in the Meadow

Tomorrow is Mother's Day. Madeline wants to give flowers to Mom. She walks to the meadow. It is a field of grass and flowers. There are many kinds of flowers! Madeline sees flowers that are very tall. They have yellow petals. They face the sun. These are sunflowers. She sees some blue flowers next. Each stem has many flowers. Each flower looks like a little bell. These are bluebells. Madeline picks some. Then she sees small yellow flowers. She can't remember what they are called. But she remembers a trick she learned. Hold it up to your chin. Does your chin look yellow? Then you like butter. Now she remembers the name. They are called buttercups.

Answer the questions below. Use the words in the word bank.

sunflower   Mom   meadow   buttercup

1. Where does Madeline look for flowers? _____

2. What flower is very tall? _____

3. What flower turns her chin yellow? _____

4. Who will Madeline give the flowers to? _____

Scary Movie

Carlos and Caroline love going to the movies. Popcorn tastes great. Sometimes they get candy, too. Today they are watching a scary movie. It's about ghosts. The ghosts live in the same house as a family. The ghosts make strange things happen. Pictures fall off the wall. The family is scared. Carlos and Caroline are scared, too! Caroline almost drops her popcorn. But soon the ghosts stop scaring the family. Everyone becomes friends. The movie ends. Then Carlos and Caroline find Dad outside. They get in the car and ride

home. Carlos tells Dad all about the movie. Dad asks them if they want to see a scary movie again. "Yes! Next Saturday, please!" they say.

Read each question. Circle the right answer.

1. Where are Carlos and Caroline?

      movies   school   kitchen

2. What is the movie about?

      giraffes   ghosts   cars

3. Who drives them home?

      ghost   Mom   Dad

4. When will they see another movie?

      never   Saturday   spring

Summer at the Seashore

It's a beautiful summer day! Many kids are at the seashore. There is the beach and the ocean. You can play on the sand or in the water. Juan runs into the waves. The water feels so cool. He swims around. Juan sees Emily swim by him. She has a surfboard with her. She lies down on it. Emily rides the waves back to the shore. Then she watches Logan. He is playing volleyball with his friends. It's hard to play in the sand! Logan gets tired. He finds his sister Sarah. She is sunbathing on a towel. Logan wants to rest, too. The sunshine feels good.

Where are they? Draw a line from each sentence to the right place.

Emily is surfing.	**on sand**
Logan is playing volleyball.	**on towel**
Juan is swimming.	**on surfboard**
Sarah is sunbathing.	**in waves**

Discover Dolphins

Dolphins need to breathe air. How can they live in the ocean? Every dolphin has a hole on its head. The hole is called a blowhole. The dolphin swims to the top of the water. The blowhole opens. The dolphin takes in air. Dolphins need to come above the water often to breathe. So they have to be good swimmers. They have flippers to help them turn. Flippers help them play games, too. You could see two dolphins playing chase! Dolphins live with other dolphins. They take care of the calves. A calf is a baby dolphin. Dolphins keep each other safe, too. A dolphin will tell another dolphin if a shark is coming.

Answer the questions below.

1. Where do dolphins live?

_____

2. What do dolphins use to breathe?

_____

3. What is a baby dolphin called?

_____

4. Who might go after a dolphin?

_____

Mr. Magic

"Boys and girls, come inside! The show is about to start!" Adrian follows his class to the school gym. But this isn't gym class. Chairs are set up in rows. Everyone sits down. A man comes on the stage. He is wearing black clothes and a black hat. He calls himself Mr. Magic. It's a magic show! First Mr. Magic takes off his hat. He puts it on a small table. Then he waves his hand above the hat. Adrian watches. Mr. Magic picks up the hat. There is a pink rabbit on the table! This is a great trick. Adrian will try it at home tonight. Adrian has a pet rabbit, too!

Read each question. Circle the right answer.

1. What does Adrian watch?

football   magic   TV

2. Where is the show?

school   bookstore   beach

3. What does the man wave?

hand   ocean   wand

4. When will Adrian try the trick?

tomorrow   tonight   Tuesday

Play with Clay

It is raining hard. Hannah must stay inside. But she can still have fun. Her mom asks if she wants to play with clay. What a great idea! She can make a mug. Hannah picks up a big piece of clay. It's hard. She presses it in her hands. She keeps pressing. The clay gets softer. Then Hannah makes a cup shape from the clay. Her brother wants to play, too. He can make the handle for the mug. He makes a long piece of clay. He presses each end to the side of the mug. Hannah puts the clay on a board. It's time to let the clay dry. Later she will paint the mug pink with red hearts!

Answer the questions below. Use the words in the word bank.

brother   board   later   mug

1. What is Hannah making? _____

2. Who is helping? _____

3. Where does she put the mug to dry? _____

4. When will Hannah paint it? _____

High in the Sky

Dad waves goodbye at the gate. Josh walks down the tunnel. He steps in. Josh finds his seat. He has never ridden in an airplane before! He wonders what it's like to fly. Soon the airplane takes off. It lifts into the sky. Josh smiles. He is going to New York City. That place is very far from his house. Grandma lives in New York City. He can't wait to visit her! Josh has never been to a city before. He wonders how tall the buildings will be. He will feel very small next to them. Josh looks out the plane window. Are those ants on the ground? No! They are cars. He feels very big up here!

Answer the questions below.

1. What is Josh riding in? _____

2. Where is Josh going? _____

3. Who will he visit? _____

4. What does he see out the window? _____

Kernels of Corn

Do you eat corn sometimes? Do you know where it comes from? The little pieces of corn are called kernels. These yellow kernels grow in rows on the corn. The whole corn plant grows in a big field. How does the corn get there? A farmer plants it. He makes rows of corn in the field. The field should get a lot of sun and rain. The corn plants grow very tall! The farmer waits until the corn is done growing. In the summer he goes to the field and picks the corn. It's a lot of work. But the kernels taste so good!

Answer the questions below. Use the words in the word bank.

> summer   kernels   farmer   field

1. Where does corn grow? _____

2. Who plants the corn? _____

3. When is corn picked? _____

4. What part of the corn plant can you eat? _____

Starry Sky

Billy likes to be outside at night. He lies down on the grass. He looks up. The black sky is full of stars. Billy sees three bright stars in a row. Those stars are called Orion's belt. Orion is a hunter from long ago. Billy read about him in his star book. Billy knows how to find different groups of stars. Over there is the Big Dipper. It is shaped like a spoon. Now Billy wants to find Draco. He looks for the shape of a dragon. There is Draco! Then Billy sees the crown. He can't remember its name. He opens the star book. He uses the flashlight to read. The crown shape is called Cassiopeia. That's hard to spell. But the stars above are easy to find!

What do the groups of stars look like? Draw a line from the name to its shape.

Big Dipper	hunter
Orion	dragon
Draco	crown
Cassiopeia	spoon

Fun Fair

School is out and the town fair is here. The fair lasts for a week in June. Alyssa's parents take her and her sister to the fair. Alyssa wants to ride the bumper cars first. Her car is hard to steer. Crash! She hits the other cars. But it's still fun! Next Alyssa runs to the Ferris wheel. She gets tied into the seat. The wheel turns. She goes higher and higher. Soon Alyssa is at the top. She can see the whole town! She likes this ride the best. Then Alyssa finds her sister. She was riding the merry-go-round. They walk to the games. Alyssa takes a water balloon. She hits the bull's-eye! Alyssa wins a teddy bear.

Read each question. Circle the right answer.

1. When is the big fair?

June   July   January

2. What ride does Alyssa like best?

merry-go-round   bumper cars   Ferris wheel

3. Where does Alyssa find her sister?

merry-go-round   bumper cars   Ferris wheel

4. What does Alyssa win?

toy car   teddy bear   goldfish

Sierra at the Stable

Sierra's cousins live on a farm. Sierra likes to visit them. They have two horses. She finds the horses in the stable. That is where they eat and sleep. One of Sierra's cousins brings some hay. It looks like straw. But the horses think the hay is yummy! Sierra touches Peaches on the nose. Peaches is brown. She has a white mane. The mane is the hair on the horse's head and neck. Peaches has a soft mane. Blackie's mane is black and shiny. He is the nicest horse in the stable. Sierra's cousins let her ride Blackie. He is very calm as they ride together. Sierra and Blackie watch the sunset. She wishes she could live on a farm, too!

Answer the questions below. Use the words in the word bank.

Peaches   sunset   hay   stable

1. What do horses eat? _____

2. Who has a white mane? _____

3. Where do horses sleep? _____

4. When does Sierra ride Blackie? _____

Frog Facts

"Ribbit! Ribbit!" You know when you hear frogs. But it's not so easy to see them. Frogs can be green or brown. They can be any color that helps them hide. Frogs surprise the bugs they eat. Frogs have long legs. Their back legs are very strong. Frogs can jump far on land! But frogs are born in the water. A mother frog lays eggs in a pond or stream. The eggs hatch and tadpoles come out. Tadpoles look like little fish. They live and swim in the water. Soon the tadpoles grow into frogs. The frogs hop out of the water. Then they live on land. Listen for frogs in the spring. That's when they sing the most. "Ribbit!"

Answer the questions below.

1. What do frogs eat?

_____

2. Where do tadpoles live?

_____

3. Where do grown frogs live?

_____

4. When can you hear frogs sing the most?

_____

Camping at the Lake

Andrew is camping with his family this weekend. They are camping near a lake. It is very warm and peaceful. Andrew wants to swim. They must set up the tent first. He helps his father with the tent. This is where they will sleep. Now they can have fun! Andrew runs to the lake. But the water is too cold for swimming. Andrew watches nature instead. He listens to the birds. He sees a squirrel eat an acorn. There are many animals to see. Soon it's time for dinner. They cook hot dogs in a fire. Then they go to sleep in the tent. Andrew wakes up early. He takes a picture of the lake. He wants to remember it.

Read each question. Circle the right answer.

1. What kind of trip is Andrew on?

hunting

camping

swimming

2. Where does Andrew sleep?

bed

grass

tent

3. What does Andrew do first?

set up the tent

swim in the lake

eat a hot dog

4. What does Andrew do last?

watch nature

take a picture

take a bath

In the Dentist's Chair

Some kids are afraid of the dentist. But Destiny isn't scared. She brushes her teeth two times a day. Her teeth are clean and strong. Destiny has fun at the dentist's office. She lies down on a big chair. It is very soft. She watches the TV on the wall. A cartoon is on! Then her dentist comes in. First, she cleans Destiny's teeth. Next, the dentist looks close. Are there any holes in her teeth? No, there are none. Then the dentist hands a cup to Destiny. It has pink water. Destiny swishes it in her mouth. It tastes like bubblegum! The best part is at the end. The dentist gives Destiny a blue balloon.

Answer the questions below.

1. Who is Destiny unafraid of? _____

2. What does Destiny watch? _____

3. What does the dentist do first? _____

4. What does Destiny get at the end? _____

Sandwich Steps

Would you like a grilled cheese sandwich? Here is how to make one! Get bread, cheese, and butter. Take two slices of bread. Put a little butter on the slices. Then take the cheese. Place the cheese on one slice of bread. Put the other slice of bread on top. Then find a grown-up to help you. The grown-up should heat up a pan on the stove. Get a spatula. Set the sandwich in the pan. Be careful! The pan is very hot. Wait for the cheese to get soft. Take the spatula again. Flip the sandwich over in the pan. Watch the clock. It will be ready after a minute. Mmmm! A gooey grilled cheese sandwich tastes great!

What's the order? Draw a line to each step of the directions.

first   Place cheese between bread.

second   Flip sandwich over.

third   Put butter on bread.

last   Set sandwich in pan.

Baby Butterflies

A butterfly is a pretty bug. It has large wings. The wings can be any color of the rainbow. But butterflies aren't born with wings. A butterfly starts life as an egg. This egg sticks to a leaf. The egg hatches. A caterpillar comes out of the egg. Did you know that caterpillars are baby butterflies? The caterpillar eats the leaf. Then it crawls on branches. It looks for more leaves to eat. The caterpillar eats and eats and eats. Then it is full. Next it takes silk from its body. The caterpillar makes a cocoon of silk around itself. The cocoon protects the caterpillar. It changes inside the cocoon. One day it comes out. The caterpillar is a butterfly now!

Answer the questions below.
Use the words in the word bank.

cocoon   butterfly   egg   caterpillar

1. What does a butterfly start life as?

_____

2. What crawls on branches and eats leaves?

_____

3. What does a caterpillar make with silk?

_____

4. What comes out of a cocoon?

_____

Basketball Fall

Vicky is the best player on the basketball team. She can shoot the ball high. She gets the ball in the net almost every time. Her friend Jasmine is good at basketball, too. She is a fast runner. Today they have a basketball game. Jasmine dribbles the ball down the court. She passes the ball. Vicky catches it. She jumps high. The ball goes through the net! But something is wrong. Vicky's foot hurts a lot. She must have landed on it sideways. Vicky's dad takes her to the hospital. Her foot is broken. The doctor puts a cast on her foot. The cast will help her foot get better.

Read each question. Circle the right answer.

1. What is Vicky good at?

running down the court

passing the ball

shooting the ball

2. Who is on Vicky's team?

Liz

Jasmine

Sara

3. Where does Vicky's dad drive?

hospital

home

park

4. What happens at the end of the story?

Vicky wins the basketball game.

Vicky gets a cast on her foot.

Jasmine breaks her foot, too.

Ice Cream Truck

Ring-ring! Ring-ring! Is that the phone? Is it the doorbell? Christopher listens carefully. The ringing gets closer. He remembers that it's summer now. It must be the ice cream truck! Christopher rushes out of the house. The truck passes by. He has to run faster! He catches up to it. The truck stops.

Christopher wants an ice cream cone with strawberry ice cream! But he forgot to bring money. His sister Chloe runs up behind him. She has money. Chloe gives some to Christopher. She is a kind sister. They buy ice cream cones. Yum! Christopher pays her back. He puts money in Chloe's piggy bank.

Answer the questions below.

1. When does the ice cream truck come? _____

2. Who runs to the ice cream truck first? _____

3. Who gives money to Christopher? _____

4. Where does Chloe keep her money? _____

First Day of School

Owen stands in front of his house. It feels strange to carry a backpack again. Owen didn't carry one in the summer. Now it's September. Today is the first day of school. Owen is waiting for the yellow bus. Soon he sees it coming. It stops for him. Owen steps on. There are so many other kids. They are talking and laughing. Owen looks for a seat. Are there any left? He finds the last seat. It's next to Austin! Owen hasn't seen Austin since June. They talk about summer break. Austin went to Florida. The bus stops in front of the school. The kids walk off the bus and smile. It's a new year!

Read each sentence. Circle *yes* or *no*.

1. School starts in September.   yes   no

2. Owen walks to school.   yes   no

3. Austin went to Florida on summer break.   yes   no

4. Kids are sad that day.   yes   no

Better Make the Butter!

Do you like butter on your toast? Do you like it on a baked potato? Butter makes food sweet and creamy. Do you know how butter is made? It starts with a cow that makes milk. A farmer milks the cow. He catches the milk in a pail. Then he lets the milk sit. Soon cream rises to the top. The farmer takes the cream off the milk. The cream is thick and yellow. Next the farmer puts the cream in a tub. He churns the cream. This means that he stirs it slowly. He churns for a long time. The cream gets thicker and thicker. Now it's butter! But the butter is very soft. He puts it in a cold place. Soon the butter is hard and ready to eat.

What's the order? Draw a line to each step of the directions.

first   Churn the cream.

second   Milk the cow.

third   Put the butter in a cold place.

last   Take the cream off the top of the milk.

Surprise Party

Liz is walking home. She is sad. Today is her birthday. No one remembered! She opens the door to her house. The lights turn on. Liz jumps back. She sees her mom. All her friends are there, too. She sees a sign that says "Happy Birthday." It's a surprise party! Everyone gives her a hug. Now Liz is happy. There are many presents. She opens the biggest one first. It has a funny shape. It's a bike! Then she opens more presents. She gets some games and a dress. She says thank you to everyone. Then they begin to sing "Happy Birthday." Liz's mom brings out a cake with candles. Liz blows out the candles. Everyone gets a piece of cake. Liz takes a bite. It's vanilla cake with lemon frosting. Yum!

Read each question. Circle the right answer.

1. Where is Liz walking?

home

school

bank

2. What does everyone sing?

Happy Birthday!

Happy New Year!

Surprise!

3. What does Liz open first?

bike

dress

game

4. What does Liz do last?

sing

eat cake

dance

Ready for the Race

Mark loves to run. He can go very fast. He feels free in the wind. He will run in the big race on Monday. He needs to practice. Mark wakes up early on Saturday. First, he stretches his legs and arms. This is necessary. Mark doesn't want to hurt himself. Then he starts running down his street. He goes all the way around the block. Mark does this ten times. He's tired! But he must practice more on Sunday. Mark wakes up early again. He stretches. He runs around the block only five times today. The race is tomorrow. He needs to save some strength. Mark eats a good dinner that night. His dad makes a big bowl of pasta for him. Mark is ready to win!

Read each sentence. Circle *yes* or *no*.

1. Mark is a slow runner.   yes   no

2. The big race is on Tuesday.   yes   no

3. Mark practices on Saturday and Sunday.   yes   no

4. Runners eat a lot the night before a race.   yes   no

5. Stretching isn't necessary.   yes   no

Sick Day

Natalie opens her eyes. It is still dark in her room. Her clock says 5:00. She never wakes up early. She feels warm. Her cheeks are hot. Natalie walks down the hall to Grandma's room. Natalie wakes her up. Grandma thinks that Natalie is sick. She should stay home from school today and let Grandma take care of her. That sounds like fun! Grandma makes Natalie a small breakfast. Natalie has some juice and a piece of toast. She isn't very hungry. Then they play quiet games together. First, Grandma sets up the checkerboard. They play checkers for an hour. But Natalie loses a checker under the couch. It's time for a new game. Natalie finds her deck of cards. They play Go Fish. Natalie has fun. But she is getting tired. Grandma reads her a story in bed. Soon Natalie is taking a nap.

Answer the questions below.

1. What time does Natalie wake up? _____

2. Where won't she go today? _____

3. Who takes care of Natalie? _____

4. What game do they play first? _____

5. What does Natalie do at the end of the story? _____

Chicks and Eggs

Do you eat eggs? Maybe you had them for breakfast. But there is another kind of egg. It has a chicken inside. This baby chicken is called a chick. The mother chicken is called a hen. First, she lays an egg. The egg can be white or brown. The chick is inside. It isn't ready to come out yet. It needs to grow in the egg. The hen sits on the egg to keep it warm. She sits and sits and sits. She sits for three weeks! Then the chick is ready. But how can the chick get out of the egg? The chick must use its beak. The beak is sharp. It can poke a big hole in the egg. The egg breaks open. Out comes a fuzzy yellow chick!

Answer the questions below. Use the words in the word bank.

sit   chick   hen   beak   three

1. What is a mother chicken called? _____

2. What does she do after she lays an egg? _____

3. For how many weeks must the egg stay warm? _____

4. What first pokes out of the egg? _____

5. Who comes out of the egg? _____

Tap Dance

Hurry up! The dance show is starting in a minute. All the girls are putting on their outfits. Ella is rushing. She ties her dance shoes. The girls run behind the stage. It's very dark. They can't wait to show what they can do. The room is filled with parents. Then the music turns on. Lights shine on the stage. Here they go! Ella and the girls dance onto the stage. They tap their feet to the music. Then they start to move in a circle. They tap dance at the same time. It's not easy. Ella feels her shoe getting loose. It's untied! She could trip on the laces. Ella is at the back of the circle. She steps out and ties her shoe very fast. Then she dances back into the circle! The girls finish the song. They take a bow. The parents clap. No one saw what Ella did!

What's the order? Draw a line to each part of the story.

first   Ella's shoe comes untied.

second   The girls start to dance in a circle.

third   Ella puts on her dance outfit and shoes.

fourth   The girls bow.

last   The stage lights up.

Postcard Pal

Do you have a pen pal? Lucas does. He likes reading letters from Amber. Amber writes letters on postcards. They have pictures of a beautiful beach. That is where she lives. Lucas writes back to her. He uses postcards with pictures of his town. He always starts his letters with "Dear Amber." He learned that in school. But then Lucas writes anything he wants. Today he writes about his fishing trip. He caught a huge fish! Amber will like to read about it. Lucas must get the postcard to her. He rides his bike to the post office. That is where you can mail things. Lucas waits in line. Then he buys a stamp. The stamp shows that he paid to mail the postcard. He sticks the stamp on the corner of the postcard. Lucas drops it in the mailbox. Soon Amber will read it!

Read each question. Circle the right answer.

1. Who is Lucas writing to?

Amber

Allison

Sara

2. How does Lucas start the postcard?

Hey, Miss

Dear Amber

Hi, it's Luke

3. How does the postcard get to Amber?

Lucas takes it to her.

A bird takes it to her.

Lucas mails it.

4. Where does Lucas take the postcard?

school

post office

soccer field

5. How does Lucas pay for mailing the postcard?

He buys a stamp.

He buys a ticket.

He sells lemonade.

Don't Waste Water

Stephanie and her mom are watching TV. The news talks about water. Their town is running out of water to drink. Stephanie gets worried. But Mom knows how to save water. They look at the kitchen sink. The water is dripping. Mom turns the handle until the water stops. Next they go into the bathroom. Mom says that Stephanie can take shorter showers. Then Mom helps Stephanie check the bathroom sink. It's not dripping. Mom asks about brushing her teeth. Does Stephanie leave the water running? She shouldn't. Last they walk to the driveway. Stephanie needs to wash the car today. Mom brings her a pail. She should use the pail instead of the hose. The hose uses much more water. It's easy to save water! The town can have enough for everyone.

Read each sentence. Circle *yes* or *no*.

1. Stephanie's mom knows how to save water.　　　　　　yes　　no

2. Stephanie should take shorter showers.　　　　　　yes　　no

3. She should let water drip.　　　　　　yes　　no

4. She should run the water when she brushes her teeth.　　yes　　no

5. She should use a hose to wash the car.　　　　　yes　　no

Piano Practice

Devin likes to play the piano. The piano is in the living room. He rests his fingers on the keys. The keys are black or white. Devin presses a key. Ping! He listens to its sound. These different sounds are called notes. He knows how to make a lot of notes. Devin plays the piano almost every day. But he learns the most on Thursdays. That's when Miss Nelson comes over. She is the piano teacher. Miss Nelson teaches him a new song every week. This week Devin learns "London Bridge." He learns the notes fast. He can sing along, too! Then Miss Nelson tells him about making notes louder. She shows Devin a pedal under the piano. He should press it with his foot. Devin plays a note and presses the pedal, too. The note is loud!

Answer the questions below. Use the words in the word bank.

> pedal   finger   key   foot   Thursday

1. What day does Miss Nelson come over? _____

2. What is black or white and makes a note? _____

3. What does Devin use to press a key? _____

4. What does Devin press to make a note louder? _____

5. What does he use to press the pedal? _____

Smash!

"Catch me if you can!" Isaiah yells and runs into the dining room. He and his sister Andrea are playing tag. Isaiah races around the table. They shouldn't be playing there! That room has things that can break. Andrea runs after Isaiah. Their parents aren't home. No one will know! Isaiah is getting tired. Andrea could catch him. So he leaps under the table. He's very fast. Andrea keeps going. She runs into a wood stand. Smash! The flower vase is on the floor. It has broken into five pieces. Now they are in trouble! But Andrea has an idea. She gets some glue. They glue the pieces together carefully. The vase doesn't look broken. They put the vase on the stand. Isaiah and Andrea finish just in time. Dad is home now. They hope that he will not see the cracks!

Answer the questions below.

1. What are Isaiah and Andrea playing? _____

2. Where are they playing? _____

3. Who runs into the stand? _____

4. How do they fix the vase? _____

5. When does Dad come home? _____

Lucky Day

Angel is walking down the street. He drops his sunglasses on the sidewalk. He looks down. There is a quarter near his sunglasses. What a lucky day! Maybe he could buy a treat at the grocery store. But the quarter is next to the store's door. It might belong to someone inside. Angel goes in the store. He walks to the front desk. He asks the woman there if anyone lost a quarter. She says no. She tells him he can keep the money. Angel leaves the store. He sees the gumball machine outside. Gum would taste good. But then Angel sees a man next to the machine. He has a cup with some coins. He tells Angel that he doesn't have a home. Angel feels sad. He gives the quarter to the man. Now everyone has a lucky day.

Read each sentence. Circle *yes* or *no*.

1. Angel finds two quarters.   yes   no

2. Angel finds the money outside.   yes   no

3. No one in the store is missing money.   yes   no

4. Angel buys a gumball.   yes   no

5. Angel gives the quarter to a homeless man.   yes   no

Deep Sleep

Melanie got a new bed yesterday. It is softer than her old bed. Melanie couldn't wait to try out the bed. She turned the lights off early. She fell asleep right away. She fell into a deep sleep. Melanie started dreaming. She dreamed that she was at her aunt's house. She and her cousins were playing catch in the grass. "Buzz! Buzz!" There was something behind her. She turned. It was a huge bee! It was the biggest one she had ever seen. And it was chasing her! Melanie ran through the grass. The buzzing got louder. She looked and saw the bee was closer! She ran faster. It still got closer. She ran toward the lake. Bees can't swim. Melanie jumped in the lake. She dove deep. She was safe! But why did she still hear buzzing? She was back in her new bed. Her alarm clock was buzzing!

Answer the questions below.

1. Where did Melanie sleep last night? _____

2. Where was she in her dream? _____

3. What was chasing Melanie? _____

4. How did she get away? _____

5. What woke Melanie up? _____

All About Zebras

Do you know that zebras are a kind of horse? A lot of horses have manes and eat grass. Look closely at a zebra. It has a short mane. A zebra eats grass, too. You may know that zebras have stripes. The stripes are white and black. But sometimes the stripes are white and brown. The stripes guard the zebras from lions. The zebras stand together. Lions see so many stripes. They can't find just one zebra to chase. The zebras live together in these groups. Zebra families stay together. The baby zebras are called foals. They are very cute! Foals can run soon after they are born. Zebras are friendly to each other, too. You might see a zebra smile. This is how it says hello to another zebra!

Finish each sentence.

1. A zebra is a kind of _____.

2. Zebras eat _____.

3. The stripes guard zebras from _____.

4. Baby zebras are called _____.

5. Zebras say hello to each other by _____.

Roller Rink

Patrick isn't good at roller-skating. He falls all the time. His friend Marcy is having a roller-skating party today. Patrick is there. He watches the kids on the roller-skating rink. They skate in a circle. No one falls! He wonders how they do it. Patrick can't even stop his roller-skates. He always skates into the rink's wall. But he will not sit and watch today. He will try to have fun. Marcy will help him. Patrick skates onto the rink. Marcy skates right behind him. She will catch him if he falls. Marcy tells him to skate a little faster. Then she skates next to him. She shows him how to use the stoppers. The stoppers will help him slow down. Patrick tries them. He slows down! He didn't have to use the wall. Maybe roller-skating isn't so bad!

Read each sentence. Circle *yes* or *no*.

1. Patrick is good at roller-skating.   yes   no

2. Patrick is at a roller-skating party.   yes   no

3. Kids skate in a circle.   yes   no

4. Patrick sits in a corner.   yes   no

5. He learns how to stop his skates.   yes   no

Road Trip

The Mitchells are driving a long way. They are going across the country! It's a long car trip. They need to have plenty to do. Taylor brought a lot of books. She likes to read ghost stories. She can read for hours! Her sister Kaylee is an artist. She brought a notepad and some pencils. Kaylee draws what she sees when she looks out the window. She draws pictures with barns and cows. They will help her remember the trip. But Taylor and Kaylee get bored at night. It's too dark for Taylor to read. Kaylee can't see out the window. So Mrs. Mitchell turns on the radio. Everyone sings as loud as they can. Then the girls get tired. Kaylee falls asleep first. She sleeps with her head against the window. Taylor stays awake to listen to the music.

Answer the questions below.

1. Where are the Mitchells driving? _____

2. Who likes to read in the car? _____

3. Who draws? _____

4. When do they all sing songs? _____

5. How does Kaylee sleep? _____

Antonio's Apple

Antonio was hungry after school. He wiggled his loose tooth while he thought about a snack. Antonio picked a red apple from the fruit bowl. He sat down and took a bite. It was juicy! He ate more. Then he stood up to get a glass of milk. Antonio tried to wiggle the tooth again. But it was gone! He didn't see it fall out. Where did it go? He looked at the apple. The tooth was in the apple! Antonio called to Mom. He showed her the tooth. She said that he would get a new tooth. It would grow in the same spot. But he must put the old tooth under his pillow. Antonio did just that. He woke up the next morning. He checked under his pillow. The tooth was gone. But a dime was there! He showed Mom. She said that the tooth fairy brought it.

Answer the questions below.

1. What did Antonio lose? _____

2. Where did he find it? _____

3. Who did he tell? _____

4. Where did Antonio put it? _____

5. How did a dime get there? _____

Twenty Teeth

Have you lost any baby teeth? You have baby teeth when you are a baby. You have twenty of them. But they begin to fall out when you are about six years old. They need to make room for adult teeth. There are thirty-two adult teeth! All teeth are important. You need them to chew. You need them to speak, too. That is why you must take care of your teeth. The best way is to brush them. Use a toothbrush. Brush two times a day. You can also use floss. Floss is a kind of string. It cleans between your teeth. You should see a dentist, too.

The dentist will clean your teeth. He will check that your teeth are healthy. Visit your dentist two times a year. Keep your smile bright!

Answer the questions below. Use the words in the word bank.

| floss | two | dentist | toothbrush | thirty-two |

1. How many adult teeth will you have? _____

2. What brushes your teeth? _____

3. How many times a day should you brush your teeth? _____

4. What cleans between your teeth? _____

5. Who should you visit two times a year? _____

Read and Report

It's time to read! The school has a reading contest every year. It begins in April. Everyone in the school can enter. Kids read as many books as they can. The contest ends in May. The kid who reads the most wins the contest. The winner gets a prize. The prize is a new bookshelf. Jackie wants that prize! She needs a place for all her books. She loves to read. She likes mystery stories the best. Jackie must win the contest. She will read every night. But there is another part of the contest. She must write a short report on every book. That takes time. Jackie will write them before breakfast. She will win the bookshelf!

Read each sentence. Circle *yes* or *no*.

1. The reading contest is only for the first grade.   yes   no

2. The contest ends in May.   yes   no

3. Jackie wants a new bike.   yes   no

4. Jackie will read every night.   yes   no

5. She must write a report.   yes   no

Kitten in the Tree

Noah was walking Sadie. It was taking a long time. She was sniffing a tree. She sat down. She looked up into the tree. Then she barked! Noah heard a meow. It sounded like a kitten. But the meow was coming from above them. Was there a kitten in the sky? No. A kitten was in that tree! Noah tied Sadie to the trunk. He started to climb. He reached the white kitten. It was shaking. He picked it up and took it to the ground. Sadie came over. She sniffed the kitten. She licked it, too! Someone was missing this cute kitten. Noah took the kitten to his house. He drew posters about the found kitten. He put them on poles along his street. But no one came. So Noah kept the kitten!

What's the order? Draw a line to each part of the story.

first	**Noah put up posters.**
second	**Noah was walking his dog.**
third	**Sadie licked the kitten.**
fourth	**They heard a meow.**
last	**Noah climbed the tree.**

Dogs and Chocolate

Noah doesn't save his money. He likes to spend it on candy. He buys small chocolate candies. They are covered in shiny foil. His parents say he shouldn't have so much candy. Noah hides the candy under his bed. Then no one will know! One day Noah looks under his bed. He wants his last piece of chocolate. It's gone! Someone must have eaten it. But his parents don't eat candy. Noah has an idea. He goes outside. He walks over to Sadie's doghouse. She is not there. But he sees some shiny foil. Sadie took the chocolate! Noah calls her name. His father comes out and says that Sadie is inside. He sees the foil in Noah's hand. He asks if Sadie ate the candy. Noah's father tells him that chocolate is toxic to dogs. Chocolate can hurt Sadie. But she only ate a small piece. Sadie will be fine. Now Noah will move his candy to a safer hiding place!

Read each question. Circle the right answer.

1. What does Noah like to spend?

money   time   candy

2. Who hides candy under the bed?

Sadie   Noah   kitten

3. Where does Noah find the foil?

under the bed

on the kitchen table

in Sadie's doghouse

4. Who hears Noah calling?

his father

his kitten

his mother

5. What does "toxic" mean?

It can help you.   It can hurt you.

It tastes good.

Aboard a Boat

Boats travel on lakes and rivers. They can go across the ocean, too. How do they move? Some boats use the wind for power. These are called sailboats. The wind blows the boat's sails. The sail can be a white triangle. It is made out of sturdy cloth. Have you ever been aboard a sailboat? You might have seen the captain. The captain drives the boat. You might also have stood on the deck. The deck is made of wood. It is flat. Below the deck is the cabin. People can sleep and eat inside the cabin. There might be a bed, a small kitchen, and a bathroom there. A boat has everything you need to travel in the water!

Answer the questions below. Use the words in the word bank.

deck   sail   cabin   captain   aboard

1. What part of the boat is made of cloth? _____

2. Where can you stand and watch the waves? _____

3. What are you when you are on the boat? _____

4. Who drives the boat? _____

5. Where do you sleep on the boat? _____

Something from the City

Ding-dong! Grandma and Grandpa are here! Jesse opens the front door. He gives his grandparents a big hug. They just returned from the city. They were there on a trip. Grandma tells Jesse about all the cars and people. The city is a busy place! They went to a show in the city. People danced and sang on the stage. Grandma says it was a lot of fun to watch. Next Grandpa shows Jesse some pictures of the city. There are a lot of buildings. But there are pretty trees, too. Then Grandma tells Jesse how they went underground. There are trains under the city! They traveled on the trains. Grandma hands Jesse something. It's a special coin. It only pays for riding the underground train. Jesse says thank you. He also says that the gift was thoughtful. They remembered that Jesse keeps special coins!

Finish each sentence.

1. Grandma and Grandpa returned from the _____.

2. Grandma and Grandpa watched a _____.

3. Grandpa shows Jesse _____.

4. Grandma gives Jesse a _____.

5. Jesse says that the gift was _____.

Strawberry Picking

Alice lives near a farm. It's a pick-your-own farm. You can pick what you want to buy. The farm has pumpkins in the fall. But Alice likes to go in the summer. Summer is strawberry time! She goes to the farm with her family. They pick a lot of strawberries together. This year Alice brings two big baskets. She wants to fill them both. She needs to get started! Alice starts picking from the first row of plants. The strawberries are big and red. They will taste so good. There are so many! The strawberries are plentiful this year. Alice picks from the second row. The sun is hot. She is getting tired.

She looks down at her two baskets. She filled them both! Alice shows her brother. He filled one basket. Now they have three baskets of strawberries. They can make a lot of strawberry jelly!

Read each sentence. Circle *yes* or *no*.

1. Fall is strawberry time.   yes   no

2. Alice goes to the farm alone.   yes   no

3. Alice picks two rows.   yes   no

4. The strawberries are plentiful.   yes   no

5. Alice fills four baskets.   yes   no

Fair Share

Today Isabel is making cookies. She uses eggs, sugar, and oatmeal. Next she mixes in raisins. Then she bakes the cookies in the oven. The kitchen smells so sweet! Isabel checks the cookies. They are done baking. She lets them cool on a rack. She goes for a walk while they cool. Miguel smells the cookies from his room. He and his two friends are getting hungry. They see the cookies in the kitchen. Oatmeal cookies with raisins are his favorite! Miguel loves to eat Isabel's cookies. His friends want to try them, too. There are twelve cookies on the rack. They should only eat half of them. And Miguel wants everyone to have an equal number. First he takes half the cookies. There are six. Then he makes three piles. Each pile has two cookies. Miguel and his friends can have two cookies each. He hopes that Isabel doesn't mind!

Answer the questions below.

1. Who is making the cookies? _____

2. What does she mix in before she bakes the cookies? _____

3. Where are they cooling? _____

4. Who wants to eat the cookies? _____

5. How does Miguel give everyone an equal number?

_____

Where Wool Comes From

"Baa-baa! Baa-baa!" That is what a sheep sounds like. What would a hundred sheep sound like? It would be very loud! A sheep isn't alone often. They live together in large groups. These groups are called flocks. A flock of sheep can live in the mountains. But most sheep live on farms. They have plenty of grass to eat there. Can you tell one sheep from another? The smallest sheep are the babies. They are called lambs. The mother sheep are called ewes. The father sheep are called rams. Some rams have horns. But all sheep have fuzzy coats. The coats grow long in the spring. They produce a lot of wool. Sheep are shaved so that people can use the wool. Sometimes sweaters are made from a sheep's wool. Hats, coats, and blankets can also be made from wool. The next time you are warm and cozy on a cold day, you may have a sheep to thank!

Read each question. Circle the right answer.

1. What sound does a sheep make?

baa-baa

ribbit-ribbit

buzz-buzz

2. What is a group of sheep called?

herd   school   flock

3. What does a sheep's coat produce?

wig   wool   winter

4. What kind of sheep can have horns?

ram   lamb   ewe

5. What is made of wool?

sweater   shoes   umbrella

Brothers and Bagels

Every Friday is pizza night. Gabe loves to eat pizza. He likes it with extra cheese. But Gabe's parents aren't home tonight. Gabe is alone with his older brother. And they don't have any money. How can they have pizza? Gabe has a great idea. He can make a bagel pizza instead! Gabe cuts a bagel in half. Then he spreads tomato sauce on the flat sides. The bagels are missing something. Gabe finds a slice of cheese. He rips it into small pieces. He places the cheese on the bagels. Then his brother turns the oven on. The oven gets hot fast. His brother puts the bagels in. Gabe watches through the oven door. Soon the cheese is melting. It is dripping off the bagels. The pizza is ready! Gabe's brother takes the bagels out. But they are too hot to eat. They have to cool first. But Gabe is so hungry!

Read each sentence. Circle *yes* or *no*.

1. Gabe makes a bagel pizza.   yes   no

2. His brother spills the sauce.   yes   no

3. Gabe turns on the oven.   yes   no

4. Gabe watches the cheese melt.   yes   no

5. They can't eat the pizza yet.   yes   no

Fawn in the Forest

What a beautiful day! Spring is now here. The sun is warm. Flowers are starting to grow. Animals are running around. Julia and Faith want to go for a walk. They like to look at plants and animals. So they take a walk through the woods. All the trees are getting little green leaves. Julia sees a bird nest in one tree. They hear baby birds, too. Then Faith sees something brown. Julia and Faith walk closer. There are two animals. Faith sees that they are deer. One is very small. It doesn't have antlers. It must be

a baby. The other deer doesn't have antlers, either. It must be the fawn's mother. Julia knows that only father deer have antlers. Faith tells Julia to stand very still. Faith says they shouldn't move. They don't want to frighten the deer. They watch the mother and the fawn enjoy the day, too.

Finish each sentence.

1. Julia and Faith are walking through the _____.

2. Julia sees a bird nest in a _____.

3. Faith sees a deer and her _____.

4. A mother deer doesn't have _____.

5. Faith knows how not to _____ a deer.

A Friend's Fear

Eric's family put a pool in the backyard. He can't wait to show Jessica. She is his best friend. They play together every day. He calls Jessica on the phone. He tells her about the pool. Eric says that she should come over to swim. Jessica says that Eric should come over to her house instead. But Eric just went to her house yesterday! He wants to play in the new pool. Jessica still wants to play at her house. Eric gets mad. He hangs up the phone. He jumps in the pool. He swims fast. Then he is not so mad. Jessica calls him back. She is sorry. She knows that it is her turn to come over to his house. But she is afraid of swimming. Eric says that it's okay. He forgives Jessica. She can still come over. They don't have to swim. They will find some other fun thing to do.

Answer the questions below.

1. Who is Eric's best friend? _____

2. What does Eric want to play in? _____

3. Where does Jessica want to play? _____

4. What is Jessica afraid of? _____

5. Does Eric forgive her? _____

Time for Tennis

Tennis is a fun game. How do you play? First, you need a tennis ball. It is soft and yellow on the outside. It can bounce very high. Next, find a racket. A racket has a handle and a flat side. You hold the handle. You hit the tennis ball with the flat side. Where do you hit the ball? You hit it over the net. But where is the net? It is in the middle of the tennis court. That is where you play. The court also has lines to show you where to stand. The last thing you'll need to play tennis is another player. He or she will stand across from you on the tennis court. The other player will also have a racket. You two will hit the ball back and forth over the net. Let the tennis match begin!

Answer the questions below. Use the words in the word bank.

racket   match   court   partner   swing

1. Where can you play tennis? _____

2. What do you use to hit the ball? _____

3. How do you move your arm? _____

4. Who can you play tennis with? _____

5. What is a game of tennis called? _____

Cleaning the Beach

Aaliyah cares a lot about the earth. She wants it to stay healthy. She knows we need to keep it clean. Today she is helping to clean the beach. The beach is very dirty. There are empty cups everywhere. She sees some cans, too. Aaliyah wants to pick up this litter. Other kids are helping. Aaliyah and the kids have big garbage bags. They put on gloves. They get to work! Aaliyah picks up a lot of litter. She starts getting tired. But the beach is clean now! She looks at her watch. It says 12:00. It's time for lunch. Aaliyah takes one bag in each hand. She carries her two bags up the hill. The kids filled a lot of bags today. Now they can rest. They sit on the clean sand. Everyone has a sandwich. Then everyone throws away his or her litter!

Read each question. Circle the right answer.

1. Where is Aaliyah?

beach

garbage dump

playground

2. What is Aaliyah picking up?

shells   fish   litter

3. How many bags does she fill?

one   two   three

4. When is lunch?

12:00   4:00   2:00

5. Where do the kids eat?

on the garbage bags   in the water   on the clean sand

Locked Out!

Nate had basketball practice after school. His team was doing great. Practice ended early. Nate walked home. He pressed the doorbell two times. He heard the doorbell ring twice. No one came to the door. Where was Mom? Then he looked at his watch. She was still at work! He tried to remember where his mom hid a key. First he looked in the big bush. He got scratched. There was no key. Maybe it was under the big rock. Nate lifted the rock. All he saw was a worm. Nate didn't know where the key could be. He sat down on the mat. It was getting dark. He wanted dinner. Then Mom's car came up the driveway. She got out and asked why he wasn't inside. Nate said he couldn't find the key. She said it was right under him the whole time. The key was under the mat!

Read each sentence. Circle *yes* or *no*.

1. Nate's basketball practice ended early.   yes   no

2. Nate rang the doorbell three times.   yes   no

3. He looked for a key in the bush first.   yes   no

4. He found a key under a rock.   yes   no

5. Nate's mom came home from work.   yes   no

Answer Key

Answers to some of the pages may vary.

Page 4
1. Who made breakfast?

2. What did Anna's dad spill?

3. What did Anna eat for breakfast?

Page 5
coat
mittens
shoes
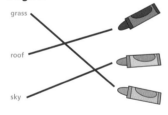

Page 6
1. Tyler rides the swing.
2. The girls play catch.
3. Mom and Dad set up the picnic.

Page 7
1. robin
2. nest
3. egg

Page 8
grass
roof
sky

Page 9
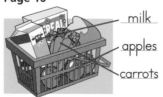

Page 10
1. Who did Mrs. Richards bring home?
2. What does Nicholas bring?
3. What is Kayla wearing?

Page 11
He is watering seeds.
It is a ripening tomato.
He is making sauce.
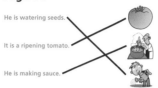

Page 12
1. Zack plants a flower.
2. His mom pulls out weeds.
3. The rabbit is taking a carrot!

Page 13
cow
pig
horse
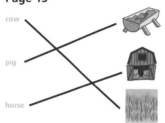

Page 14

elephant
monkey
giraffe

Page 15
1. What does a bee make?
2. What gives food to bees?
3. Who does a bee sting?

Page 16
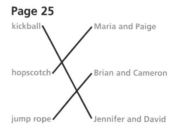
milk
apples
carrots

Page 17
1. Abigail
2. Connor
3. Jacob

Page 18
wash dishes — broom
dust — sponge
sweep floor — rag

Page 19
1. apartment
2. igloo
3. boat

Page 20
1. baseball
2. Madison
3. Lions

Page 21
1. Olivia
2. crocodile
3. Benjamin

Page 22
bread — cookie
milk — sauce
pasta — cheese

Page 23
1. forest
2. paper
3. birds

Page 24
1. boots
2. backpack
3. mountain

Page 25
kickball — Maria and Paige
hopscotch — Brian and Cameron
jump rope — Jennifer and David

Page 26
1. Saturday
2. Grandpa
3. candles

Page 27
1. meow
2. white
3. kitten

Page 28
1. Mr. Martin
2. story
3. turtle

Page 29
1. cranberry sauce
2. Grandma
3. sleep

Page 30
1. Where did Brianna go on a trip?
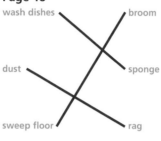
2. What did she do there?
3. When will she go home?
Tuesday   Wednesday   Thursday

Page 31
1. conductor
2. whistle
3. tracks

Page 32
Leah
Gavin
Jack
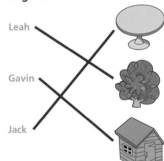

Page 33
1. Where is Sean going?

2. When is practice?
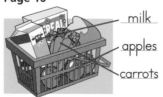
3. Who was waiting for Sean?
Dad   Mom   Grandpa

Page 34

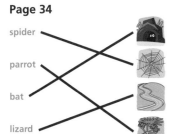

spider
parrot
bat
lizard

Page 35
1. The elephant splashes water to keep cool.
2. Elephants hug with their trunks.
3. Its trunk makes loud noises.

Page 36

1. Who goes to the circus with Evan?
Trevor   Steve   **Tom**

2. What does Evan pay?

3. Where is the clown show?

4. When do they leave the circus?
5:00   1:00   10:00

Page 37
1. beach
2. sand
3. 2:30
4. Morgan

Page 38

It is floating on water.
It is sitting on a lily pad.
It is crawling on grass.
It is swimming underwater.

Page 39
1. today
2. foot
3. field
4. goalie

Page 40

1. What took Samantha to the city?

2. When did she go there?

3. Who showed Samantha the tall buildings?
Mom   Dad   her sister

4. Where will she go after lunch?
home   **a shop**   airport

Page 41
1. Diego
2. Springfield
3. Saturday
4. yes

Page 42

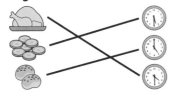

Page 43
1. ice
2. winter
3. north
4. snowman

Page 44
1. meadow
2. sunflower
3. buttercup
4. Mom

Page 45
1. movies
2. ghosts
3. Dad
4. Saturday

Page 46

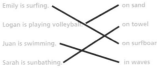

Emily is surfing.   on sand
Logan is playing volleyball.   on towel
Juan is swimming.   on surfboard
Sarah is sunbathing.   in waves

Page 47
1. ocean
2. blowhole
3. calf
4. shark

Page 48
1. magic
2. school
3. hand
4. tonight

Page 49
1. mug
2. brother
3. board
4. later

Page 50
1. airplane
2. New York City
3. Grandma
4. cars

Page 51
1. field
2. farmer
3. summer
4. kernels

Page 52

Big Dipper   hunter
Orion   dragon
Draco   crown
Cassiopeia   spoon

Page 53
1. June
2. Ferris wheel
3. merry-go-round
4. teddy bear

Page 54
1. hay
2. Peaches
3. stable
4. sunset

Page 55
1. bugs
2. water
3. land
4. spring

Page 56
1. camping
2. tent
3. set up the tent
4. take a picture

Page 57
1. dentist
2. TV
3. clean
4. balloon

Page 58

first   Place cheese between bread.
second   Flip sandwich over.
third   Put butter on bread.
last   Set sandwich in pan.

Page 59
1. egg
2. caterpillar
3. cocoon
4. butterfly

Page 60
1. shooting the ball
2. Jasmine
3. hospital
4. Vicky gets a cast on her foot.

Page 61
1. summer
2. Christopher
3. Chloe
4. piggy bank

Page 62
1. yes
2. no
3. yes
4. no

Page 63

first   Churn the cream.
second   Milk the cow.
third   Put the butter in a cold place.
last   Take the cream off the top of the milk.

Page 64
1. home
2. Happy Birthday!
3. bike
4. eat cake

Page 65
1. no
2. no
3. yes
4. yes
5. no

Page 66
1. 5:00
2. school
3. Grandma
4. checkers
5. takes a nap

Page 67
1. hen
2. sit
3. three
4. beak
5. chick

Page 68

first   Ella's shoe comes untied.
second   The girls start to dance in a circle.
third   Ella puts on her dance outfit and shoes.
fourth   The girls bow.
last   The stage lights up.

Page 69
1. Amber
2. Dear Amber
3. Lucas mails it.
4. post office
5. He buys a stamp.

Page 70
1. yes
2. yes
3. no
4. no
5. no

Page 71
1. Thursday
2. key
3. finger
4. pedal
5. foot

Page 72
1. tag
2. dining room
3. Andrea
4. glue the pieces
5. after they glue the vase

Page 73
1. no
2. yes
3. yes
4. no
5. yes

Page 74
1. new bed
2. aunt's house
3. huge bee
4. jumped in lake
5. alarm clock

Page 75
1. horse
2. grass
3. lions
4. foals
5. smiling

Page 76
1. no
2. yes
3. yes
4. no
5. yes

Page 77
1. across the country
2. Taylor
3. Kaylee
4. night
5. with her head against the
   window

Page 78
1. tooth
2. apple
3. Mom
4. under his pillow
5. The tooth fairy brought it.

Page 79
1. thirty-two
2. toothbrush
3. two
4. floss
5. dentist

Page 80
1. no
2. yes
3. no
4. yes
5. yes

Page 81

first — Noah climbed the tree.
second — Noah was walking his dog.
third — They heard a meow.
fourth — Sadie licked the kitten.
last — Noah put up posters.

Page 82
1. money
2. Noah
3. in Sadie's doghouse
4. his father
5. It can hurt you.

Page 83
1. sail
2. deck
3. aboard
4. captain
5. cabin

Page 84
1. city
2. show
3. pictures
4. coin
5. thoughtful

Page 85
1. no
2. no
3. yes
4. yes
5. no

Page 86
1. Isabel
2. raisins
3. rack
4. Miguel and his friends
5. He makes equal piles.

Page 87
1. baa-baa
2. flock
3. wool
4. ram
5. sweater

Page 88
1. yes
2. no
3. no
4. yes
5. yes

Page 89
1. woods
2. tree
3. fawn
4. antlers
5. frighten

Page 90
1. Jessica
2. pool
3. her house
4. swimming
5. yes

Page 91
1. court
2. racket
3. swing
4. partner
5. match

Page 92
1. beach
2. litter
3. two
4. 12:00
5. on the clean sand

Page 93
1. yes
2. no
3. yes
4. no
5. yes